MMA Mastery
Flow Chain Drilling
and Integrated O/D Training

Mark Hatmaker

MMA Mastery #1

Cover photo by Mitch Thomas
Interior photos by Doug Werner

Tracks Publishing
San Diego, California

MMA Mastery
Flow Chain Drilling and Integrated O/D Training
Mark Hatmaker

Tracks Publishing
140 Brightwood Avenue
Chula Vista, CA 91910
619-476-7125
tracks@cox.net
www.startupsports.com
trackspublishing.com

Publisher's Cataloging-in-Publication

Hatmaker, Mark.

    MMA mastery : flow chain drilling and integrated O/D training / Mark Hatmaker ; cover photo by Mitch Thomas ; interior photos by Doug Werner. -- San Diego, Calif. : Tracks Pub., c2010.

    p. ; cm.
    (MMA mastery ; #1)

    ISBN: 978-1-884654-38-1
    Includes index.

    1. Mixed martial arts--Training. 2. Hand-to-hand fighting--Training. I. Werner, Doug, 1950- II. Title. III. Title: Mixed martial arts mastery: flow chain drilling and integrated offensive / defensive training. IV. Series: MMA mastery ; no. 1.

GV1102.7.M59 H38 2010   2010926575
796.815--dc22   1006

Books by Mark Hatmaker

No Holds Barred Fighting:
The Ultimate Guide to Submission Wrestling

More No Holds Barred Fighting:
Killer Submissions

No Holds Barred Fighting:
Savage Strikes

No Holds Barred Fighting:
Takedowns

No Holds Barred Fighting:
The Clinch

No Holds Barred Fighting:
The Ultimate Guide to Conditioning

No Holds Barred Fighting:
The Kicking Bible

No Holds Barred Fighting:
The Book of Essential Submissions

Boxing Mastery

No Second Chance
A Reality-Based Guide to Self-Defense

MMA Mastery:
Flow Chain Drilling and Integrated O/D Training

MMA Mastery:
Ground and Pound

Books are available through major bookstores
and booksellers on the Internet.

Dedication

To anyone and everyone who escapes the trap of the confirmation bias. We must strive, always, not to shape the research, but to allow the research to shape us.

Acknowledgements

Phyllis Carter
Kylie Hatmaker
Dan Marx
Jackie Smith
Mitch Thomas
Shane Tucker

Warning label
The fighting arts include contact and can be dangerous. Use proper equipment and train safely. Practice with restraint and respect for your partners. Drill for fun, fitness and to improve skills. Do not fight with the intent to do harm.

Contents

How to use the No Holds Barred Fighting (NHBF) and Mixed Martial Arts (MMA) Manuals

This book and the others in this series are meant to be used in an interlocking synergistic manner where the sum value of the manuals is greater than the individual parts. What we are striving to do with each manual is to focus on a specific aspect of the twin sports of NHB/submission wrestling and give thoughtful consideration to the necessary ideas, tactics and strategies pertinent to the facet of focus. We are aware that this piecemeal approach may seem lacking if one consumes only one or two manuals at most, but we are confident that once

three or more manuals have been studied the overall picture or method will begin to reveal itself.

Since the manuals are interlocking, there is no single manual in the series that is meant to be complete in and of itself. For example, although *NHBF: Savage Strikes* is a thorough compendium on NHB/self-defense striking, it is bolstered with side-by-side study of *Boxing Mastery*. While the book *NHBF: Killer Submissions* introduces the idea of chaining submissions and can be used as a solitary tool, it becomes stronger with an understanding of the material that preceded it in the first submission manual.

And so on and so forth with each manual in this series. So let's dive into the world of MMA competition and discover how to emphasize that most important word in Mixed Martial Arts — Mix.

Mark Hatmaker

Introduction

The following story is from *The Analects of Confucius.* While traveling with his student, the Master asked, "Ssu, do you take me for one who studies much and remembers it all?" The student replied, "Yes, is that not so, Master?" The Master replied, "No, I link all knowledge upon a single thread."

Wisdom is found not in quantity of information ingested, but by quality of said information and (perhaps more importantly) integration of the quality information.

That exchange, in a nutshell, is what this volume is about — linking all MMA knowledge upon a single thread. At the risk of being pedantic and overexplain the lesson in Confucius' homily, the crux of the opening quote is: Wisdom is found not in quantity of information ingested, but by quality of said information and (perhaps more importantly) integration of the quality information. I risk your impatience by breaking this down even further.

On the subject of information quality, it is only quality information that passes muster. The world is chock full of information. You can literally Google or Wiki any subject and have reams of information at your disposal. This is a boon for civilization, but there are also minuses to this plenty. The primary minus is that all information is not equal. Equity is measured by the twin judges of veracity and utility.

Verifiable information is manna — there are few intellectual errors worse than operating on incorrect data. Configuring the Hubble Telescope would be impossible if we still accepted the paradigm that the earth is at the center of the universe. The search for and development of new antibiotics in the treatment of disease and infection would be discounted if medical science still labored under the misapprehension of "spontaneous generation" to explain how maladies arise in the human body. And fighters would be woefully ill-prepared to enter the ring or cage if they accepted the nonsense of touch (or worse yet) "touchless" knockouts. Accurate information is the foundation upon which mighty structures can be built.

Once we have verified the information at hand, we must test if for utility. In other words, ask if the given information applies to our life or task at hand. The fact that Kevin Federline gained a few extra pounds after his divorce from Britney Spears may be true, but it will serve us not a whit if our goal is to fix a carburetor or fight a better fight. This is an asinine example, I know, but it is the very pith of the lesson — not all facts are relevant. We all too often err when we mistake encyclopedic facts taken out of context as wisdom, intelligence or "smarts." We all know people who, although "book smart" (and that is an admirable thing to be), lack what is known as good old everyday common sense. We do not want to be the Ken Jennings on Jeopardy who seems to have every fact in the world at our disposal (unless our goal is to be a Jeopardy champion, then that is a fine role model, indeed). In our own arena, we don't need to be the fighter who knows every submission that ever existed or every striking combination that has ever been thrown. As contrary to wisdom as it sounds, we don't need this sort of encyclopedic knowledge of the given field to be successful.

Paradoxically, we want to strive to become the fighters who test a technique for veracity and then for utility. This subject is covered in great depth in our volume *NHBF: The Book of Essential Submissions.* Once the tests of veracity and utility have been aced, we must progress to the hardest, but most rewarding task of all — that of learning to link all our information upon a single string. That is what this book is about.

We want to assist you in threading the needle with accurate and useful knowledge and then weaving that thread into one united tapestry of effective offense and defense.

We want to assist you in threading the needle with accurate and useful knowledge and then weaving that thread into one united tapestry of effective offense and defense.

The First "M"

Before the advent of Mixed Martial Arts, individual combat arts/sports could be easily subdivided into categories akin to biology's taxonomic system (life, domain, kingdom, phylum, class, order, family, genus, species). You could put Judo in the grappling column, various Karate styles under striking, and Tai Chi, well, you figure that one out. These distinct and separate entities/species existed in their own little habitats seemingly unaware or unconcerned with the methods of approach to similar problems that other species might take. All that seemed to matter was the purity of the species.

In the early 1990s with the renaissance of MMA competition, that ignorance (willful or not) became harder and harder to maintain. Via MMA competition, we began to see species set against species in survival of the fittest contests.

This full bore adoption and adaptation of successful strategies by competing entities was and is the best thing that has, can, and will happen to this wonderful sport.

Initially there were some clear winners and losers — Brazilian Jiu-jitsu (BJJ) yes, Ninjutsu, not so much. After a while these separate entities began to take notice of one another's successful traits and, just as in biologic evolution, began to merge, adapt and recombine qualities. This is evolution on a quick scale in the world of ideas.

This full bore adoption and adaptation of successful strategies by competing entities was and is the best thing that has, can, and will happen to this wonderful sport. Improvement comes not from closed systems, but from open systems willing to always look beyond what is in the current system's DNA, as it were. Closed systems are subject to failure at some point. Let's look more closely at MMA's quick evolution to see this closed system failure in bold relief.

At MMA's inception in the early 1990s, we saw the inherent superiority of grappling systems, submission grappling in particular, with BJJ at the top of the food chain. We also saw hard-core striking hold sway with Muay Thai elbows, knees and low kicks being a bit more successful than straight, above-the-belt kickboxing. We, in turn, witnessed what was not successful — low to zero grappling emphasis, esoteric striking arts and high-stanced boxing among other things. Those who mastered the successful techniques won, and those who didn't were weeded out along with their less effective arsenals. That brings us to the middle period of MMA's current history.

This middle period saw athletes far savvier about grappling and striking, showing a willingness to cross-train in arts/sports outside their domain of preference. This cross-training took the form of "I'm a BJJ man or Muay Thai fighter or _____, but I also train _____ to round out my game." These cross-training fighters of the middle period brought us the familiar sight of grapplers striking just enough to close the distance and strikers knowing just enough grappling to stay out of or get out of trouble.

The newest period in MMA history (and by my estimation the most interesting) is the fighter of today. This fighter seems to have no "specialty," no art to which fealty must be pledged. This fighter strikes well, shoots well, grounds and pounds well, submits well. This fighter is so well-rounded across all discrete modes of the sport that one is hard-pressed to know what art/sport to label him on "The Tale of the Tape" (and here's hoping that outdated bit of info falls by the wayside soon).

We are looking at a new era of MMA athletes who see MMA as a distinct sport unto itself. They do not have the compartmentalized mentality of the older athletes. We are looking at athletes for whom the most important word in Mixed Martial Arts is Mix. More and more athletes are doing more things well across a broader range of skills, and this is an exceptionally exciting development in the sport.

This equality of skill across ranges is far more successful (and desirable) than specializing in one area. And it is far more unpredictable than the middle-period athletes who switched gears between one or two arts with one of the arts holding obvious preference. The new era reveals the breed of athletes who will carry this sport forward. These athletes train, not with an eye on the past (ancient or recent), but rather on the future. The best fighters will learn to blend all elements of MMA into one cohesive whole with no single aspect holding more or less importance than the other. It is with an eye on aiding this mix that this manual has been devised.

> We are looking at athletes for whom the most important word in Mixed Martial Arts is Mix.

This manual is meant to be a tool to remove the separation of elements and to unite them into integrated drill sets so that stylistic distinctions can be transcended. To aid this effort, we must not see the fight as a series of separate elements, but as a congruent whole where each and every aspect is linked to one another whether it be striking, shooting, grappling or submission work.

Open versus Closed Systems

To expand on a theme, closed systems are predictable, open systems (complex systems) are subject to low to zero predictability. Let's look at climate on a micro and macro scale to illustrate. First, the closed system.

If you have central heating in your home, the mere act of adjusting your thermostat allows you to predict the climate in your home with a high degree of probability. Assuming your thermostat is in working order, doors and windows are closed and no steaming shower is running for hours, you can predict the temperature in each room to within a few degrees of accuracy. Presuming no gaping holes in the roof, chances are for zero precipitation. The Weather Channel broadcast for your home would be exceptionally boring. Let's zoom out a bit and look at an open system, the climate of a geographical region. We have far more factors to consider: seasonal time, barometric pressure, the amount of humidity the air is carrying, surface albedo, wind speed and direction, location on the globe and a myriad of other factors working in a baffling welter of shifting interdependencies. This weather forecast is subject to variability and might be accurate only a few days out. Even these predictions can be startlingly wrong (as many of us with washed-out weekend plans can attest). The greater the number of variables, the lesser the predictive power.

The best fighters will learn how to blend all elements of MMA into one cohesive whole with no single aspect holding more or less importance than the other.

Back to the subject at hand, single combat arts (those with no mix) are closed systems. Let's use the formidable Russian art of competitive Sambo as our grappling example. Sambo's closed rule set allows no strikes and no head attacks (no choking or cranking). Thus we see heavy emphasis on grappling and a beautifully complex ground game with a deep vocabulary of leg locks since the head has been prohibited as a target.

We can predict with some degree of accuracy that the winner in any given match will come by way of arm or leg lock, presuming a submission finish and not a win via points.

We'll use boxing as our striking closed system example. Presuming the fight does not go to the judges, the fight will

> Rather than approach each aspect of the fight (striking, shooting, clinch work, riding, ground and pound, submissions) as separate unrelated entities (individual closed systems), we need to see them as unified contributions to the whole.

be decided by punches to the body or head. As soon as we take either of the above closed system arts examples and add some variables, the game plan changes exponentially. Simply add one new element to boxing, say, knees to the body, and the clinch becomes a whole new animal. Add head attacks to Sambo, and a vast majority of the leg attacks dissolve because turning the back to an opponent is not the best of ideas. When you add variables, it makes less sense to train in a pure, specific manner.

An MMA fight is more akin to an open system than to a closed one. Rather than approach each aspect of the fight (striking, shooting, clinch work, riding, ground and pound, submissions) as separate unrelated entities (individual closed systems), we need to see them as unified contributions to the whole. In a closed system, attention to one or two variables is all that is needed for comfort. You can set your thermostat and close the doors of your house and get what you expect. But there is not a competent meteorologist on the planet who would dare to take only one or two data sets (today's temperature and wind speed) and tell you what's going to happen 10 days from now (well, maybe Al Gore). No, the more complex the system, the more open it is, the more variables we need to take into account. We need to see the variables not as separate sums added to a simple calculation, but as shifting data sets that need to be reconfigured with each move in a single variable.

MMA competition is an open system and needs to be understood as such. With the knowledge that it is an open system, we not only witness it as such, but also use this information to train for it by scrupulously avoiding closed system approaches. We need to adopt open system methods that better replicate what actually occurs in the rings and cages of the world.

Integration versus cross-training

Oh, this poor flogged horse. Please, Mark, not another analogy? Afraid so.

Think back to when you were learning to speak your native language. Can't remember can you? But I think it's safe to say that your parents were wise enough to avoid compartmentalization. They taught you by immersing you in the language itself. They spoke directly to you, perhaps in abbreviated sentences or with a limited vocabulary, but they, nevertheless, spoke in complete sentences. They also spoke in front of you taking no pains to limit grammar, vocabulary or the complexity of their sentence structure. They did not segment, isolate or cross-train you in language arts. Your parents were educational geniuses.

Imagine where your language skills would be if your parents had taught you as language is usually taught in school. Rather than simply speaking to you, immersing you in the language, they insisted on separating the individual words of the language into separate categories for individual study — nouns, verbs, adjectives, adverbs, conjunctions, prepositions and the like. What if rather than speaking contextually about what was going on in your environment at the moment, say, around the dinner table ("Please pass the salt."), they chose to have you ignore your present circumstances and parrot sentences that lacked context ("My suitcases are in the hotel where I may purchase stationery.")? What if your parents subdivided even further and drilled you on declarative sentences on Mondays, interrogatives on Wednesdays and interjections on Fridays? How do you think your spoken communication would have progressed under such a pedagogical approach?

I wager that the above examples strike you as a ludicrous way to teach language to a child. Yet somewhere along the way this de-contextualizing of information into discrete bits and keeping them separate until some magical recombination in the future has become the standard.

The hybrid drilling we introduce in this manual is presented the way your parents taught you to speak. We begin with short sentences without isolating individual parts of speech and gradually progress through more sophisticated forms of communication. At no point do we dwell on a singular aspect of the game. You do not converse in daily life using only nouns or verbs. We should not spend time in our sports training with needless compartmentalization.

Cross-training makes sense if (and only if) you are preparing for a multi-sport event such as a triathlon where the individual skills are performed in a singular/linear manner. You must train to run, to swim and to bike because these events are performed separately, not as some unusual mixed triathlon where you must sprint with your bike into the water and then pedal while submerged. This would change the timbre of triathlon training altogether.

Mixed Martial Arts is not a linear sport. You do not box, then compete in Muay Thai competition and then freestyle wrestling and then add a Greco-Roman event followed by a Brazilian Jiu-jitsu match. MMA is far more sophisticated than that. Preparing for the sport as if it were a linear event might be as shortsighted as teaching a child to speak not by actual speech, but by diagramming sentences. I submit that integration in training is the way. Leave the cross-training to the actual multi-sport athletes — we are dealing with a far more complex animal in MMA.

The hybrid drilling we introduce in this manual is presented the way your parents taught you to speak.

And for those who think they spot the error in my thinking, noticing that I neglect focusing on each "range" of the fight, read on.

The Myth of Ranges

There is a school of thought (actually many schools) within the combat arts/sports that posits that a fight (any fight) can be examined and then deconstructed into specific range delineations. These ranges can, well, for lack of a better word, range from as few as four to as many as 10. Keep in mind we are talking about unarmed confrontations in this range discussion.

I'll be honest. I cut some slack to the range believers who err on the side of lower numbers, but the higher we go, the more it seems like intellectual hairsplitting or post-workout

Mixed Martial Arts is not a linear sport. You do not box, then compete in Muay Thai competition and then freestyle wrestling and then add a Greco-Roman event followed by a Brazilian Jiu-jitsu match. MMA is far more sophisticated than that.

shoot-the-bull musings than reflections of reality.

Let's define a couple of the more standard range ideas before we begin to look at what actually occurs in a fight. The more grounded range theories (the lower the number the better) state that there are four ranges in a fight: kicking, punching, trapping and grappling. These are fairly self-explanatory, but for clarity's sake, let's define them.

Kicking range
You and your opponent can reach one another with a kick, but not a punch.

Punching range
You and your opponent can reach each other with punches, but are not yet within clinching or grappling range.

Trapping range
You and your opponent are close enough to use a series of hand immobilizations to launch inside striking attacks.

Grappling range
Yes, it's all self-explanatory at this point.

Some of the higher range number systems include long punching range (jabs and other straight punches), close punching range (tight hooks and uppercuts) and H-K-E range (head-butts, knees and elbows). Grappling is separated into upright and ground work. Some make allowances for the grounded situation (one fighter is down, the other is on his feet); some include blind spot as a range (simply maneuvering behind your opponent); and you may even come across the psychological range (which means an attribute or characteristic of the conflict).

Don't get me wrong, I understand the allure of fine tuning fight analysis to such a degree that we can disentangle the various violent threads and therefore have a more complete understanding of the game in question. But are we simply adhering to arbitrary designations that bear little resemblance to reality? Is much of this range talk merely playing semantics with proxemics? And, perhaps most importantly, if there are indeed ranges, does the study of them as separate entities do us more harm than good?

Let's tackle the more sensible (by my thinking) four range system first.

Range One: Kicking

Yes, kicking can and does occur in a fight, but we do not see it simply at an outside range (there's that word) where the longest limb supposedly holds sway. We see kicking in the middle of punching exchanges. We see short choppy kicks delivered inside the clinch. We see heel chops used by grapplers on the ground, and of course, we see devastating kicks delivered by both fighters in a "grounded" range. So where exactly does the kicking range begin and end? If it can present itself anywhere, is it really a range?

Range Two: Punching

The same thing can be said here. Antagonists punch while

on the ground, they punch inside the clinch, and they punch while in some semblance of the standard definition of "punching range." We also see competitors in today's MMA punching from waaaaayyyy outside with the "Superman Punch." If the punch is as ubiquitous as the kick in a fight and presents itself across a wide variety of positions and situations, is punching, in and of itself, really a range?

Range Three: Trapping

To be honest, I just don't see it. Yes, we have all witnessed some beautifully executed trapping demonstrations, drills and even trapping combative responses. But these all seem to occur inside the constructs of an agreement. Meaning, "We will fight within this trapping range and we will both agree that trapping is to be our method." When the rule set is expanded, as we see in MMA or even on security tapes, trapping, at least so far, isn't presenting itself unless we broaden the definition to include punch muffling, arm drags and other hand controls used by grapplers. With this dearth of demonstration of the standard definition of trapping within the fight, an argument can be made that this may not be a range at all, even by the accepted definition of range.

Range Four: Grappling

This is often relegated to groundwork or work inside the clinch, but we see many a talented competitor take a fast shot from the outside, which seemingly would be boxing or kicking ranges. Just as we see strikes within "grappling ranges," we see grappling within "striking ranges."

At first glance, you would think that elbows and knees are merely inside range tools (can't get away from that word). But we have seen too many flying knees from way outside and knees and elbows on the ground end fights to confine these formidable weapons to one launching area. Again, if each and every tool that defines a so-called range presents itself across all or a majority of the other ranges, is the concept of ranges valid? A more pointed question might be, is the range concept doing a disservice to training for some?

If there are indeed ranges, does the study of them as separate entities do us more harm than good?

I think it might be a disservice in some instances. If one accepts the concept of ranges (whatever number you choose) as dogma, one will have a tendency to train in a segmented compartmentalized fashion — a sort of *We do this here and we do this technique if the fight is here* and so on. It might be a bit wiser to accept a fight (competitive or survival) for what it is — an amalgam of chaos as one fighter seeks to assert his or her strengths upon the other in whatever manner he can.

It is wise, however, to work each aspect that precedes range in most range theories. That is, work your kicks, work your boxing, work your grappling, work your shooting, work whatever tools are most likely to contribute to your game or survival. But strive to lose the artificial construct of a range for each tool. By sloughing off these seemingly unsupported ranges of a fight and moving toward full range integration (sorry about that word ... again), we move closer to reality (or at least what exhibits itself most commonly as of this writing). We also might unlock a bit more creativity in applying these formidable tools that have no need of a leash called "range."

While we're demolishing artificial walls ...

It might be a bit wiser to accept a fight (competitive or survival) for what it is — an amalgam of chaos as one fighter seeks to assert his or her strengths upon the other in whatever manner he can.

The Folly of Style

Those of us who went through a stage of watching *Enter the Dragon* obsessively will recall the scene where we find Bruce Lee on a boat making a journey to Han's island. He is approached by one of the other tournament competitors and is asked, "What's your style?" This hallmark question went on to be echoed in martial arts films too numerous to count, and in a case of life imitating art, martial artists the world over began to query one another with the same question. But is the answer to this question meaningful outside of polite curiosity? Have we inflated the word "style" in combat arts/sports to designate something more than it actually does?

To address the question of style, we must first define what style actually means. The common usage in martial arts denotes a particular mode of approach to combat situations whether in the sporting sense or street usage. We seem to think that by hearing the style tag, we will be able to divine what the individual's inculcated response will be in certain situations (and, perhaps to some degree, this is true). Those with a Tae Kwon Do style can be expected to kick well, and those with a Brazilian Jiu-jitsu style can be expected to have a good ground game. But no matter the answer, would the question be more usefully phrased as "What's your sport?"

Are we making inapt determinations when we ask what your style is? Yes, all combat can be characterized by one-on-one striking/grappling, but are we getting at what we really mean by inquiring as to style?

Let's look to other sports for a moment. A vast number of team and individual sports use a ball of some sort. When an athlete proclaims that he plays a ball sport, we may ask what his sport is. Whether he answers football, tennis, rugby, jai alai, polo, what have you, all we've learned is what individual sport he participates in. That's all. In the context of ball sports, we don't immediately jump to *Oh, he plays polo and polo is better than tennis, but not as good as rugby.* Each ball sport is what it is within the context of its own rule set and method of play. Comparative judgments regarding efficacy versus other ball sports are meaningless since we don't have (not yet, at least) MBS (Mixed Ball Sports) where tennis competitors square off against volleyball players.

This sort of interrogative does not occur within individual ball sports. In other words, an individual sport like football does not subdivide its mode of play so distinctly that it becomes a discrete entity unto itself. We don't hear of Shaolin style football squaring off against Portuguese football.

Asking a martial artist "What's your style?" informs us simply of what sport he plays and gives us a ballpark idea how that game is indulged. These side-by-side comparisons among sports only make sense in Mixed Martial Arts (MMA) where the word "mix" is what the game is all about. But even as the sport evolves, we see fewer matchups in the style versus style sense and more blending of style where MMA becomes its own style/sport. This is exactly as it should be. MMA has its own rule set and mode of play, and the strict rule sets of any other combat sport are not necessarily all one needs to make the transition to MMA. After all, as effective as boxing, kickboxing, Muay Thai, wrestling and BJJ are in and of themselves, you no longer see a straight down the line participant of a single style/sport dominate.

This blending and sloughing off of stylistic pretensions is a good thing by my way of thinking. Style within an individual sport with a restrictive rule set is terrific, and no real value judgment should come into play in a comparative sense. Tae Kwon Do players should not expect to do well in a BJJ tournament and vice versa. But when we allow style, which is a compartmentalized way of thinking and acting, to make claims into areas where mixing and blending is paramount (MMA and self-defense), then there's trouble. We would find it ludicrous for a tennis champion to assume that he can play defensive line in the NFL because his tennis game is so awesome. It wouldn't work the other way around, either.

If you are concerned with style, I urge you to think of it in the strict sporting context and to pursue it as an expression of the sport you have chosen to play. If your goals are more encompassing (MMA/self-defense), then it is wise to shed stylistic concerns and move to a technique-by-technique evaluation with no concern as to what style developed said technique. This sort of non-stylistic prioritization was espoused by Bruce Lee when he said, "Absorb what is useful and reject what is useless." My own inelegant endorsement is, "Don't bring a badminton racket to a rugby game."

The Jack-of-All-Trades is the Master of One

Apologies if that heading comes across a bit faux-deep a la The Matrix-style musing. It helps address our next point. MMA seems to be evolving away from "masters" of a single art and toward good athletes who are not great at any one thing, but pretty damn good at many things.

Have we inflated the word "style" in combat arts/sports to designate something far more than it actually does?

As already pointed out, you used to see experts/champions in individual arts with a high utility rating hold sway in MMA — arts like BJJ, wrestling and Muay Thai. But now we are seeing athletes with perhaps only half the skill in a single area as some of the past champions. Yet some of these rightly esteemed single (or dual art) competitors are seeing their posteriors handed to them on a silver platter by the dilettante upstarts. As you can guess from our repetitive theme, the answer lies in the ability of this new class of athletes to exhibit competence across a wide array of circumstances. This new breed of athlete is making the case for being a diversified novice.

Let's look to another area of physical endeavor to see this principle of diversified novices at work in an equally successful manner. There is a relatively new resurgence of thought about physical conditioning that strives to reintegrate all physical attributes (strength, endurance work, explosiveness) into one cohesive whole. This school of thought disdains isolation and cross-training as in triathlon style linear sports training, or "I did biceps yesterday and calves today" approaches. This approach to conditioning training eschews artificial separation and exercises with no corollary in reality. In other words, there is little need for isolation preacher curls in actual active life circumstances, whereas pull-ups rate high on a functional conditioning utility scale. These functional approaches to conditioning reap tremendous results and hold a high transfer percentage across many sports. You might have gathered, I'm a big fan of this empirical approach. I bring up these sorts of approaches not to tout them (and they should be touted), but to set up another analogy.

Cross-Fit, perhaps the best known of these integrated functional fitness approaches, holds a tenet of interest at its core. It is surmised that some of the strongest, fittest functional athletes in the world come from three core sports: Olympic-style weight lifting, short-to-mid distance sprinting and Olympic class gymnastics. It is reasoned that the Olympic weight lifter works with little isolation work and yet hefts impressive weight totals in the most ballistic of manners that also holds a functional correlate to real-world strength challenges.

After all, as effective as boxing, kickboxing, Muay Thai, wrestling and BJJ are in and of themselves, you no longer see a straight down the line participant of a single style/sport dominate.

Olympic sprinters display impressive speed, muscular development and endurance. Olympic class gymnasts also display impressive strength and endurance in the control of their own bodies. Each class of athlete must work for years and years to reach the upper tiers of competition. So much focus is required that the single sport must be their primary target at all times.

The tenet in question presumes that rather than devoting oneself to only one of these sports and risk developing the attributes of a single endeavor, that your attention be diversified across all three elite activities. The tenet posits that by striving to become a competent (or even a skilled) novice or intermediate athlete at all three sports, you may not develop into a world champion in any single endeavor, but you will build a considerable amount of conditioning across the widest variety of elite functional conditioning planes.

This is exactly the approach I advocate in your MMA drilling — the talented novice. You do not have to be the best boxer, the best shooter, the best Muay Thai fighter or the best BJJ player to compete successfully in MMA. At any rate, time is not on our side. Consider all the years required to pursue elite level skills in boxing, Muay Thai, freestyle wrestling, Greco-Roman wrestling, Judo, Brazilian Jiu-jitsu, Catch Wrestling or Sambo. If we assume it takes a conservative five years to master a single endeavor, and if we choose only three arts to master, we are asking an athlete to devote 15 years of his life to develop competency across the necessary circumstances of the fight. Ludicrous!

The way of the talented novice begins to make more sense in the area of efficiency (relative time expenditure). What about efficacy? I've quoted him before and I will again. The late and highly esteemed (rightly so) Jiu-jitsu master Carlson Gracie said, "Punch a Jiu-Jitsu black belt in the face once and he becomes a brown belt, punch him twice and he becomes a purple belt." Mr. Gracie's quote beautifully illustrates two points. First, by training for the fight with only one goal in mind (grappling in this instance), the introduction of another approach can cause entropy. We've seen this entropy across all planes of circumstances. Those without a ground game are easy prey for the wrestling and submission specialists of the world; the boxers who have never experienced a leg kick fall hard, and so on.

The second bit of wisdom hidden inside Mr. Gracie's quote is cloaked in a bit of seemingly negative criticism. We can take the quote to mean that the introduction of punches means the entropic devaluing of a single sport, or that one needs to train even harder in BJJ and get even more advanced to overcome the introduction of the punch. We also can take it to mean (and this is how I see it) that the introduction of the second sport (the punch) distills the first art (BJJ) to its essentials. The punch does not render BJJ ineffective, it merely strips away concepts and techniques that might hold value in BJJ versus BJJ competition. The punch reduces the art to high percentage ideas that hold higher utility for coping with the it. In other words, the advanced black belt arsenal is corralled down to a novice-to-intermediate range to better deal with the mixed sport environment.

> Non-stylistic prioritization was espoused by Bruce Lee when he said, "Absorb what is useful and reject what is useless." My own inelegant endorsement is, "Don't bring a badminton racket to a rugby game."

We see this stripped down to effective essentials across all combat sports introduced into MMA. The beautiful footwork, slips, fades, bobs and weaves of the professional boxer get reduced to good punching technique and 3-point combinations once leg kicks and the takedown are introduced. Wrestling's highly stable square and staggered stances for shooting purposes must be retooled in the face of strikes. Wrestling's dominant riding game must be stripped down in the presence of submissions. Across the board, advanced techniques in all of the pertinent arts/sports are jettisoned in favor of the basics plus a few intermediate ideas.

> We can train harder and harder at fewer things to get better and better — faster.

Honestly, when is the last time someone won a high level competition with a strike that had never been seen before? Shoot a take-down heretofore unknown to the world? Submitted someone with a move that had only been dreamt of?

In essence, MMA competition has culled each of the pertinent component sports to bare minimums. That's a good thing because it allows us the opportunity to refine our goal sets to pursue the title of the hard-core novitiate. We can train harder and harder at fewer and fewer things to get better and better — faster. And to facilitate this progress, there are no separation of elements. Just one sleek drilling method that educates hard-core essentials and unites them into the distinct and separate sport that it is.

Pareto's Principle, the Bellagio Hypothesis and the Heriarchy of Utility

If any of that heading strikes you as unfamiliar, I urge you to read a previous book in this series *NHBF: The Book of Essential Submissions*. That volume introduces the science of fight metrics as it applies to MMA competition and provide extensive breakdowns of what tactics, techniques, and strategies do and do not prove effective in cage and ring environments.

All of the drills in this book are informed by this research and contain no personal preferences or "pet moves." On the contrary, you will find nothing but tried and true, tested and proven concepts connected in logical causal links. Again, if there are any questions as to why some aspect of the game was or was not included in a given drill, I refer you to the aforementioned book.

Down & Out Drills

It's time to get to the entertainment portion of our program.

● Down & Out Drills are chain drills that link the main aspects of the fight into one cohesive whole.

● Down & Out Drills will always obey the offensive gambit/defensive counter/repeat formula and follow each link from the first fired punch to a logical end result.

● Down & Out Drills are designed to mimic the broad parameters of a fight, and when performed up to speed, will often resemble a highlight reel.

● Down & Out Drills build an appreciative amount of sport specific conditioning while developing applicable skill sets at the same time.

● Keep in mind that these drills can branch out and see other permutations at any link in the chain (Bad Libs — more on this later), but the key is to start with preestablished common scenario ready material before moving to complex skill set interjections.

● Down & Out Drills are the most plentiful drill set in our curriculum as they combine all material from the Utility Core.

● We will spend little time instructing individual technique (links in the chains) as we have covered technique in past volumes. We will provide detail only when the technique or concept is new.

● The Down & Out Drills presented here are only the tip of the iceberg, but they should provide a good template to build a comprehensive skill set and spawn self-generated chains.

Down & Out Drill protocol

● You will use five-minute rounds as the industry standard.

● You will build each chain in a link-by-link manner devoting an entire round to each link (more if a complex skill is to be seated). Building includes starting from link 1 and progressing to the current link.

● Anytime you find a glitch round (a round where your brain doesn't quite catch up to the material) repeat that round until all systems are go. Doesn't matter if it's one more round or 200, get it right. If you don't take the time to get it right, the nature of Down & Out Drills will ensure someone's gonna get thumped hard as the links progress.

● Donning all appropriate safety gear is a must because once we approach fluidity and up the contact, there will be bumps and bangs.

● Always "mean the drill." In other words, once drilling partners' learning curves are equivalent, really mean that jab, really try for that shot, really slap on that choke — make your opponent earn the drill, don't hand it to him. Not meaning the drill is a disservice to you both.

Down & Out Drill approaches
You can drill in one of two ways.

1. Feeder/Responder
In this version, one fighter is designated the Feeder, and he will lead with the first technique throughout the entire round. Example: Fighter A fires Technique 1 and Fighter B

responds with the given Counter. This format continues with Fighter A leading the charge with zero deviation. Feeder/Responder is ideal for novices and/or seating new drills.

2. Tit for Tat
This version of drilling has the fighters trade initiating roles in the midst of each individual round. Example: Fighter A fires Technique 1, Fighter B responds with the given Counter. Then Fighter B fires Technique 1 and Fighter A responds with the given Counter. Tit for Tat is ideal for the intermediate to advanced fighter as entropy will leak into the system and fighters will begin to "lose their place" within the context of the drill (who's firing/who's responding). When this entropy occurs, as it will, the key is to respond no matter what, not to drop the hands and say, "Whoops!" Use the drill to seat skills and let the escalation of speed and chaos blend naturally to a bit of scrimmage.

Down & Out Drill legend
Drills are notated in the following style. This quick primer will get you up to speed.

● Each individual link is a complete drill round.

● Fighters are designated A and B.

● Fighters "read their parts."

● Each link will build on the previous parts.

● The plus sign (+) indicates material to be added to the fighter's part from the previous link.

● Each Down & Out Drill (an entire multi-link set) will be

given a numerical heading with the number always spelled out, e.g., DRILL ONE.

● Confused? It'll make sense in a minute.

Bad Libs

Bad Libs are, in effect, short linked drills that can be inserted into the middle of a preexisting Down & Out chain. Bad Libs allow you take previously mastered material and "remix" new ideas/techniques to keep the material fresh or to address areas of concern.

● Bad Libs will be designated by Arabic numerals, e.g., BAD LIB 1.

● You will be directed where to insert Bad Libs as in the example: "Insert BAD LIB 2 into DRILL FOUR at the Double-Leg Takedown."

● Do not treat Bad Libs as separate chains — always drill from the beginning of the original Down & Out chain all the way through the Bad Libs insert.

● Let's get started and I think you'll be up and running in no time.

DRILL ONE

LINK 1
Fighter A: Jab
Fighter B: Catch

LINK 2
Fighter A: + Cross
Fighter B: + Cover
● When covering, remember to take your head to your hand and not your hand to your head. Moving your hand opens the body to attack.

Bad

Good

LINK 3
Fighter A: + Hook
Fighter B: + Cover

LINK 4
Fighter A: + Feint shoot
● Feint the shot with a change in elevation.

Fighter B: Match level
● You can thwart many leg shots by matching an opponent's level change.

LINK 5
Fighter A: + Set collar and underhook

● Always overhook the collar with your lead hand (jab hand).
● Your underhook need be no further than your palm on his shoulder blade.

LINK 6
Fighter A: + Angle / underhook and post

● Take a step toward your underhook side while shifting your collar palm to post on the near side of his face — shove hard.

LINK 7
Fighter A: + Knee

LINK 8
Fighter A: + Bar and chancery drop
● Maintain your underhook.

● Overhook his head with your post arm.

● Back step with your overhook side foot while pivoting on your underhook foot.

● At the same time, elevate with your underhook and wrench his head toward the mat to drop.

LINK 9
Fighter A: + Flat crank
● Cinch your head wrap tighter.

● Pull on his underhooked shoulder for contrary motion.

● Keep his back on the mat as you turn to look over your head-side shoulder.

LINK 10
Fighter A: + Chin hook crank
● Grip his chin with your overhook hand.
● Sit out toward his head while pulling his underhook shoulder.
● Do not allow his back off of the mat.

LINK 11 ➡
Fighter A: + Turn the corner short arm bar
● Release his chin and lean into his underhooked shoulder.
● Pop up to your feet and go toward his back placing your free-hand shin against his back and your underhook calf stepped in front of his face.
● Fall to your back hitting the short arm bar.

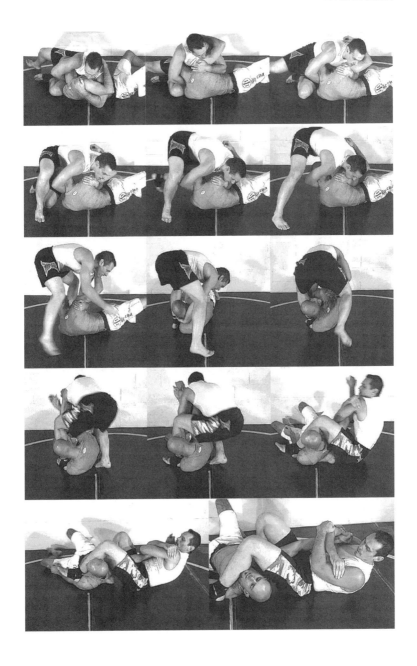

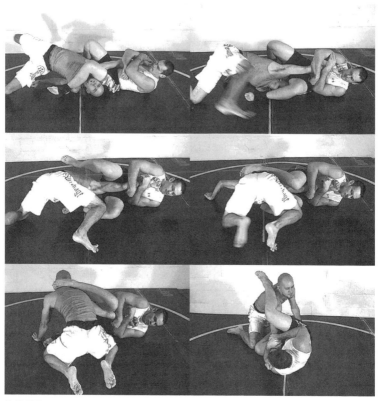

LINK 12
Fighter B: + Outside roll
● Post on your free shoulder and roll to the outside (away from Fighter A) by first swinging your near leg followed by your far leg.

● This will bring you to your knees where you can then vacuum your arm from jeopardy.

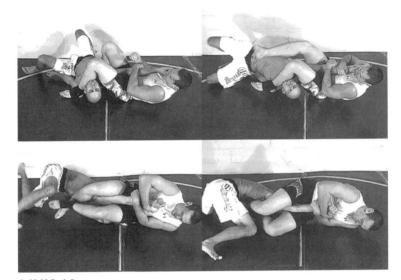

LINK 13
Fighter A: + Cross-body arm bar belly down
● As you feel Fighter B's body leave contact with your shin, roll toward your head-side shoulder and overhook his body with your hip-side leg for the full arm bar.

BAD LIB 1

Add as LINK 7 in DRILL ONE.

LINK 1
Fighter B: + Drive versus underhook and post
● Drive for the takedown.

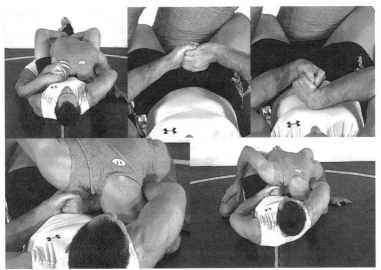

LINK 2
Fighter A: + Bottom scissors guillotine — both shoulders on the mat

● If you are dropped with both shoulders on the mat, overhook his head with your collar arm and hit a standard guillotine.

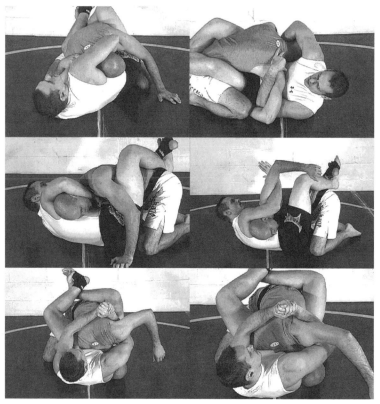

LINK 3
Fighter A: + Bottom scissors 1/2 stocks crank — underhook control shoulder on the mat
● If you are dropped with your underhook shoulder to the mat, overhook his head with your collar arm and underhook his near arm. ● Pull on his arm with this new underhook while crunching his head down with a combination lat flex and side crunch.

LINK 4
Fighter A: + 1/2 Stocks turnover
● From the 1/2 stocks position, place an elevator with your head-side control leg.
● Use your underhooks to drag his body toward your chin while kicking your elevator to the sky.

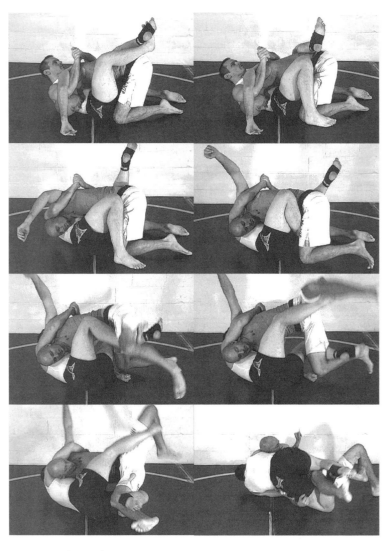

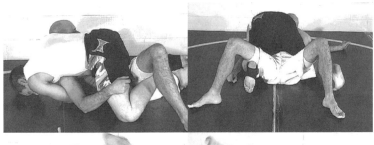

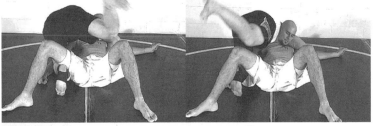

LINK 5
Fighter A: + Sit-out stocks

● Once he is turned, follow the turn and sit-out on the underhook control opposite his head.

● Slide your hips toward his head while cranking his chin toward his chest with your back. Go slow, this hits hard.

LINK 6
Fighter A: + Belly down reverse short arm bar — knee block face, chancery shoulder down

● If you are dropped onto your chancery shoulder, post on that shoulder and bring your underhook side leg over his back.

● Post this knee against the near side of his head as you strive to go belly down.

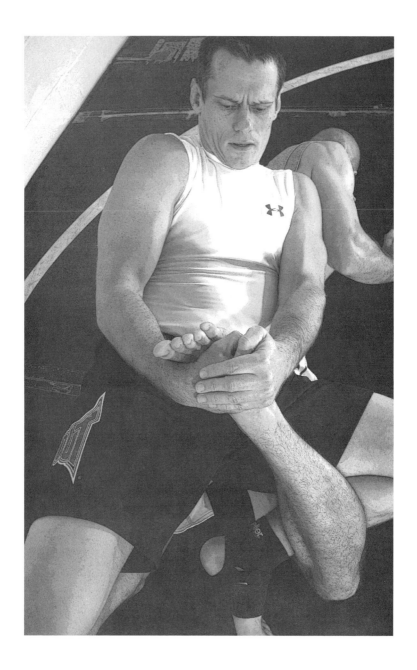

DRILL TWO

LINK 1
Fighter A: Jab
Fighter B: Catch or cover

LINK 2
Fighter B: + Jab
Fighter A: + Catch

LINK 3
Fighter B: + Cross
Fighter A: + Cover

LINK 4
Fighter B: + Lead hook
Fighter A: + Cover

LINK 5
Fighter A: + Lead hook
Fighter B: + Cover

LINK 6
Fighter B: + Rear leg kick
Fighter A: Evade or check

LINK 7
Fighter A: + Jab / clinch reach
● Use the jab to bridge the distance and seek a double-collar tie-up.
Fighter B: + Catch

LINK 8
Fighter B: + Collar and elbow control

● Counter the reach for a double-collar tie-up with a collar and elbow control. Notice that the MMA collar and elbow is slightly different in that you must control the elbow from the inside to prevent strikes — never control from the outside.

LINK 9
Fighter B: +
Collar and over-
hook snapdown

Not good — Because Mark (top man) did not pressure Dan's right arm, Dan was able to grab the leg.

LINK 10
Fighter B: + Go-behind to elbow side and leg pry
● An elbow-side go-behind must be performed as following to prevent the bottom man stopping your progress with a leg grab.

● Replace your elbow hand with the back of your collar hand.

● Use the back of this hand as a pivot point and spin around to his side.

● Pry by leaving the back of your pivot hand in place and driving his arm forward.

● Also place the back of the hip-side hand along the inside of his far thigh. Do not seatbelt him — this leads to a higher counter-vocabulary for the bottom man.

LINK 11
Fighter B: + Head-side hook to head
Fighter A: + Cover

59

LINK 12
Fighter B: + 1/2 Rotary tilt and turn the corner
● To 1/2 rotary tilt, extend your thigh pry arm as if you could lift his far leg with that arm only.
● Lay your chest onto his back while turning the corner toward his head.

LINK 13 ➡
Fighter B: + Cross-body double wrist lock (DWL)
● As you turn the corner, hook a figure-4 grip on his top arm and hit the DWL.

LINK 14
Fighter B: + DWL block
● Grip trunks or your free hand if you can to block the DWL.

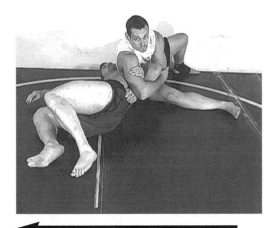

LINK 15
Fighter B: + True keylock

● Versus a blocked DWL, hug his attacked arm by releasing your figure-4 grip and ...

● Keeping your head-side arm inserted in the crook of his arm, grab your own hip-side deltoids.

● Keep his attacked wrist caught in the crook of your hip-side arm and grip the biceps of your head-side arm.

● Lean on his attacked arm and hop over his head to a sit-out on the far side of his body.

● Squeeze your arms together and take his elbow toward his head to tap.

BAD LIB 2

Add as LINK 11 in DRILL TWO.

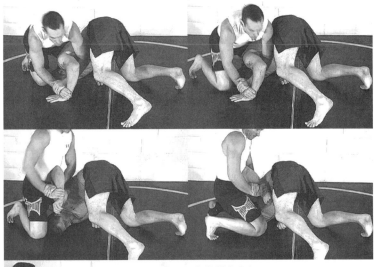

LINK 11
Fighter B: + Dorsal lock

● Hook a figure-4 grip on his top arm as you stop at his head on your knees.
● Pinch his head between your knees.
● Pull his arm toward his head to remove slack.
● Take his palm toward his back.

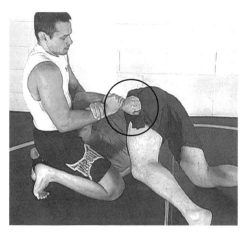

LINK 12
Fighter A: +
Dorsal block
● Block with a trunk grab or grabbing your own hand.

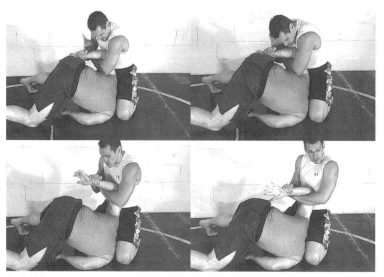

LINK 13
Fighter B: + Elbow dig
● To open his block, use the elbow of your chest-side arm to dig into his ribs.
● Once he has responded to the pain, hit the dorsal.

LINK 14 *Fighter B: + Head scissors*

If your opponent is resistant to the elbow dig …

● Fall toward his back keeping his head between your knees.

● Scissors your legs with your top leg crossed over the bottom leg (never the reverse as this can be countered with a peel).

● Straighten your legs and arch your hips while ripping/pulling his attacked arm. ● Roll toward his chest for extra "kick."

DRILL THREE

LINK 1
Fighter A: Jab
Fighter B: Catch

LINK 2
Fighter A: + Cross
Fighter B: + Cover

LINK 3
Fighter A: + Hook
Fighter B: + Cover

LINK 4
Fighter A: + Shoot
*Fighter B: + Collar and
overhook*

LINK 5
Fighter A: Drive
Fighter B: Fall to bottom scissors while hooking an arm-included

● Arm-included guillotines are more likely occurrences than clean guillotines — see *The Book of Essential Submissions* for support.

● To tighten with an arm-included, grip as deeply as you can manage with your arm-included arm and apply pressure mainly to the exposed neck.

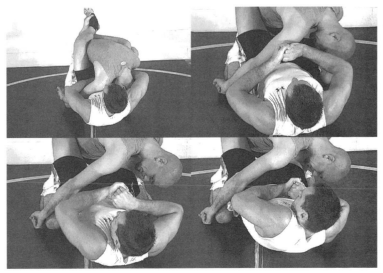

LINK 6
Fighter B: Grind turn arm-included guillotine
● Grind toward his included arm — grinding the other way accomplishes nothing.
● To do this, think driving your head-encircling wrist though his throat while arching toward his arm-included side.

LINK 7 ━━━━━━━━━━━━━━▶
Fighter B: Wizzer and step-out
● Post your arm-included-side foot on his near hip.
● Post your head-encircling elbow on the mat.
● Using your wizzer as the pivot point, step out to top position.

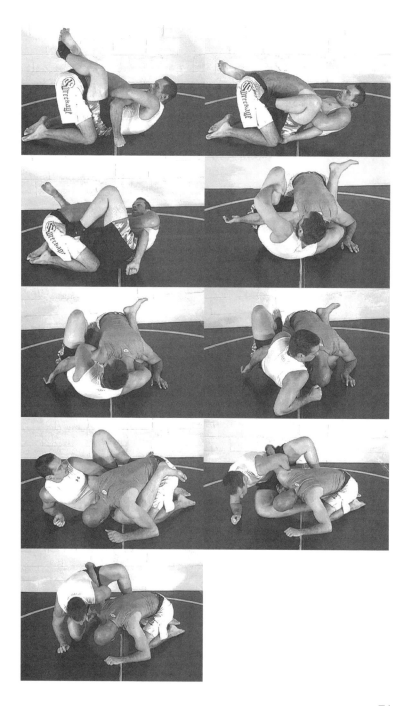

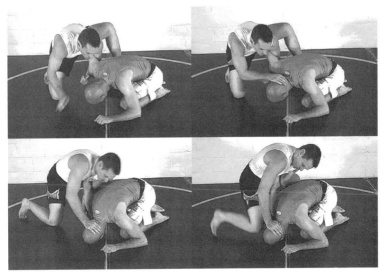

LINK 8
Fighter B: Wizzer and step-out to knee

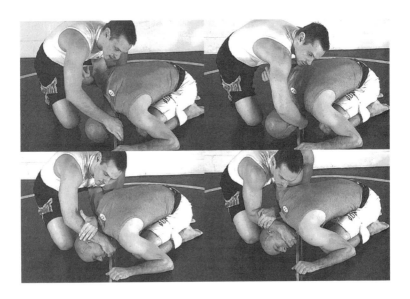

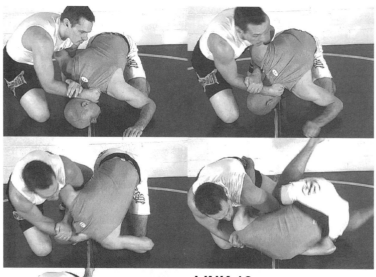

LINK 10
Fighter B: Missed chin hook to standard 3/4 Nelson

● Place the head-hand on the back of his head.

● Grip your head-control wrist with your wizzer hand.

● Drive his head down with your head control hand while …

● Driving your wizzer toward his head.

LINK 9
Fighter B: Wizzer and step-out to 3/4 Nelson with chin hook

● Grip his chin with your head-encircling hand.

● Grip the chin hook with your wizzer hand.

● Drive the wizzer arm toward his head while pulling on his chin to tap.

LINK 11
Fighter B: Ground knee
● Once you've turned him with the 3/4 Nelson, keep his head controlled and drive your head-side knee into his face.

LINK 12
Fighter B: Turn the corner short arm bar — underarm
● Post on his head with your head-control hand.
● Using this post as a pivot point, travel to the far side of his body.
● Hit the short arm bar. In this version, his attacked arm will be under your arm from the wizzer grip.

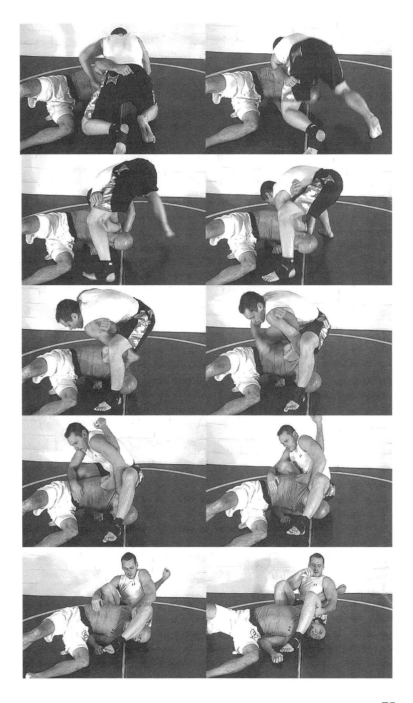

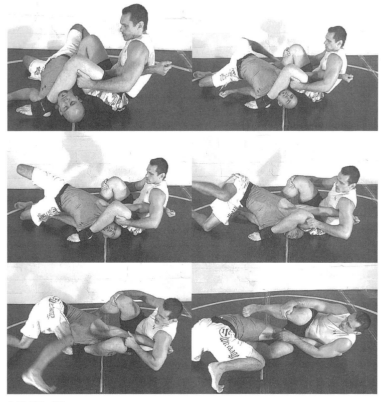

LINK 13
Fighter A: Outside roll

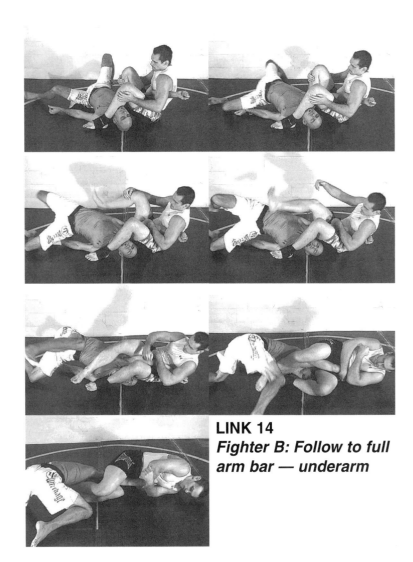

LINK 14
*Fighter B: Follow to full
arm bar — underarm*

BAD LIB 3
Add as LINK 8 in DRILL THREE.

LINK 8
Fighter B: Missed wizzer to butt scoot
● Here, you can't get the wizzer set deep, so you post on the mat with your head-control hand and scoot your butt from your opponent as much as possible.

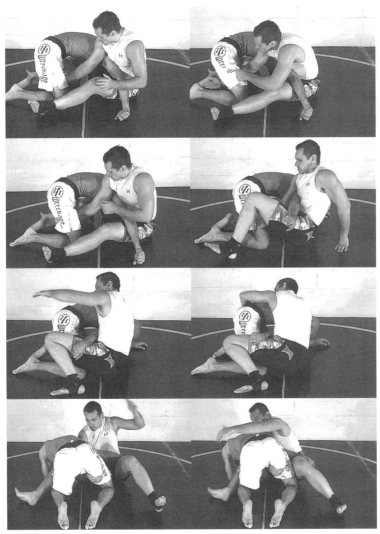

LINK 9
Fighter B: Butt scoot to switch
● Overhook his wizzer arm with the back of your other arm.
● Use the palm of this arm to reach for his inner thigh on the same side.
● Using his thigh as a ladder rung and the back of your arm as a pivot point, hit your switch.

LINK 10
Fighter B: Butt scoot to switch pry, punch and tilt
● Once you've got your switch, hit a pry on his far thigh with your non-switch hand.
● Use your switch hand to begin hooking/hammering his head.

BAD LIB 4

Here we introduce a Bad Lib within a Bad Lib. Add as LINK 9 in BAD LIB 3.

LINK 9
Fighter A: Sprawl versus the switch
● Simply sprawl the hips away denying the switch any purchase.

LINK 10 (pages 82 and 83)
Fighter B: Missed switch to power switch
● Strive to bring the far leg underneath his body to your attempted switch side. ● Set the instep of this foot against his near inner thigh. ● Keeping the back of your attempted switch arm against the back of his arm, grip your own elevating thigh.
● Pull on your thigh while kicking toward the ceiling.
● Turn toward him and hit a cross-body ride.

◄──────────────────

LINK 11
Fighter B: Cross-body pound
● Once in cross-body, begin hammering the head with back elbows and/or hammer fists.

BAD LIB 5

Another Bad Lib within a Bad Lib. Add as LINK 9 in BAD LIB 3.

LINK 9
Fighter B: Missed switches to armpit drag
● He's sprawled against the initial switch, and this sprawl blocks your power switch leg. So …
● Use the back of the attempted switch arm to strike the back of his arm hard.
● At the same time aggressively turn into your opponent for a quasi go-behind.

LINK 10
Fighter B: Armpit drag to sit-out arm bar
● This supposes that your armpit drag can't get you on top for the go-behind.
● Keep his near arm by underhooking it with both of your arms.
● Slide your hips away from him perpendicular with his shoulder.
● Lift his arm, slide your hips away and keep the armpit to armpit pressure to tap.

LINK 11
Fighter A: Bend the arm to defend the arm bar
Fighter B: DWL turnover to cross-body DWL
● Hook a double wrist lock and guide the arm over his head to turn him to his back and finish.

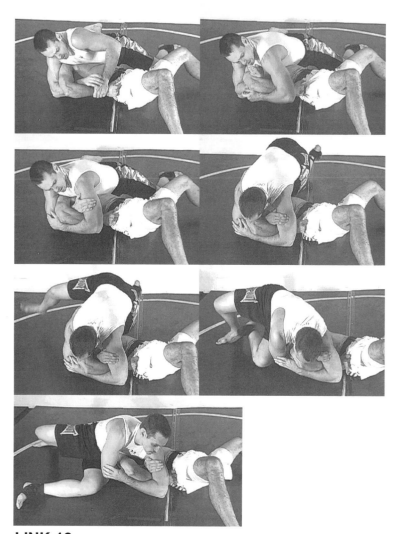

LINK 12
Fighter A: Trunk grab to block the DWL
Fighter B: Transition to keylock

BAD LIB 6

Yet another Bad Lib within a Bad Lib. Add as LINK 9 in BAD LIB 3. By this point you should understand how to branch logical progressions ad naseum, always linking new skills while reinforcing high utility movement.

LINK 9
Fighter A: Drive
● As your opponent shoots for the sit-up butt scoot …
● Drive into him hard as if shooting a tackle to return him to his back.

LINK 10
Fighter B: Knee bump bottom scissors DWL
● As you are driven back, go with the fall and …
● Use your knee/top of your thigh (in this case the left knee) to strike his right upper arm, handing if off for you to hook a DWL.

LINK 11
Fighter A: Trunk grab to block DWL

LINK 12
Fighter B: Armpit drag
● Versus his trunk grab, keep your DWL hook-up and hit the armpit drag. Use this momentum to rise to your butt.
● At this point you insert Bad Libs 3, 4 and/or 5 or …

LINK 13
Fighter B: Underhook gut wrench
● Drive your drag arm underneath his stomach.
● Overhook his waist with your far side arm.
● Grip your hands.
● Slide your crotch tight to his near knee (allowing distance between your hips and his knee denies you power and leverage).
● Arch toward your outside shoulder while lifting him over your body to dump him to your left to attain cross-body control.

LINK 14
Fighter A: Sprawl to block the underhook
● As Fighter A strives to underhook your body, sprawl to block his arm.

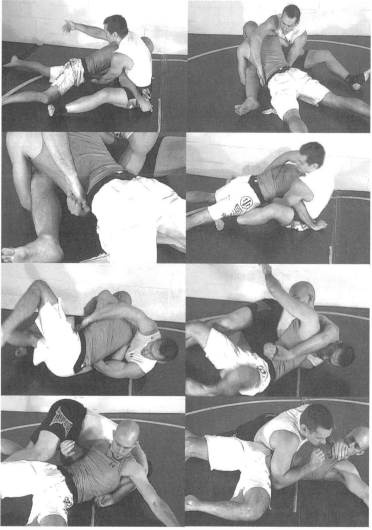

LINK 15
Fighter B: Overhook gut wrench
● Beat his sprawl block by overhooking his waist with your drag arm.

● Your outside arm will still be able to underhook his waist.

● Grip your hands and perform the gut wrench with this alternate grip. ● Hit cross-body control.

DRILL FOUR

LINK 1
Fighter A: Jab
Fighter B: Catch

LINK 2
Fighter A: + Cross
Fighter B: + Cover

LINK 3
Fighter A: + Lead hook
Fighter B: Cover

LINK 4
Fighter B: Shoot double leg

LINK 5
Fighter A: Retreat and set collar and overhook

LINK 6
Fighter A: Hook chancery
● Overhook his head with your collar control arm and turn his face toward your overhook arm with your fist.
● Your collar-forearm will be braced on his face not on his throat.
● Grip your overhook forearm with your head-control hand.
● Use the crooks of your arms to shuck his head to the center of your chest, not with his head underneath your armpit.
● Keeping your elbows tight to your body, stay low — there will be no lift.
● Squeeze your arms tight to your sides while popping the back of your wrist up and into his face.

LINK 7
Fighter B: Pop arm out of chancery
● Swing your overhooked arm back and toward your hip to clear his overhook.

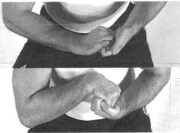

LINK 8
Fighter A: Old school guillotine
● Keep his head in the center of your chest and your head-control hand just where it was — palm down.
● Finger hook grip your hands — keeping the head-control hand in palm-down position.
● Keep your elbows tight to your body and stay low — there will be no lift.
● Squeeze your arms tight to your sides while popping the back of your wrist up and into his face.

BAD LIB 7

Here are a few links to be inserted at LINK 7 of DRILL FOUR.

LINK 7
Fighter B: Drive to release overhook
● Drive your overhooked arm into him as if to tackle and to break the hook chancery.

LINK 8
Fighter A: Gator choke
● Maintain head control after his drive.
● Hit an armpit drag with your former overhook arm.
● Grip the forearm (not biceps) of your drag arm with your head-control hand.
● Drive over your head-control shoulder. *Continued next page.*

99

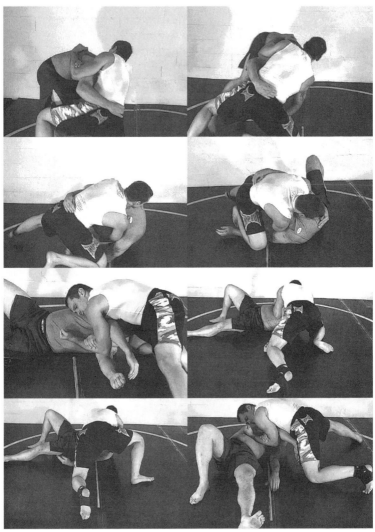

● As you roll out on top, tighten your grip and travel toward his hips.

DRILL FIVE

LINK 1
Fighter A: Cross
Fighter B: Cover

LINK 2
Fighter A: Hook
Fighter B: Cover

LINK 3
Fighter A: Cross
Fighter B: Cover

LINK 4
Fighter B: Shoot double leg

LINK 5
Fighter A: Retreat and set collar and overhook snapdown

LINK 6
Fighter B: Surge

● Rather than get caught on the bad side of a failed takedown or pull bottom scissors/guard, you can surge.

● As you are snapped, post both hands to the mat.

● Quickly step your unloaded foot (rear foot) in line with your hands — it can be between the hands or to the outside.

● Arch your back as if looking to the sky were the most important goal in the world.

● Return to your feet.

LINK 7
Fighter A: Outside hook / rear knee
● As Fighter B surges, keep your collar hand in place — this is your outside hook.
● Snap/pull his head toward your opposite knee. Pulling to the same side knee allows your opponent to easily shrug out.

LINK 8
Fighter A: Hook chancery

LINK 9
*Fighter B: Pop arm out
of chancery*

LINK 10
*Fighter A: New school
guillotine*
● Use the standard bar grip
beneath the chin.

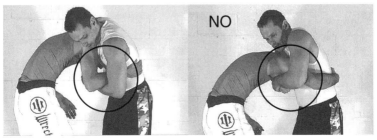

NO

LINK 11
Fighter B: Insert a wedge
● This is the only defense you need versus a new school guillotine (standing or on the ground). ● Insert your far side arm (arm opposite the head attack) into the crook of his same side arm. ● Penetrate only far enough to rest your upper forearm on his forearm. ● Drive your forearm down to deny him leverage for the guillotine.

LINK 12
Fighter A: Block the wedge
● As he seeks the wedge, simply tuck your attacking elbow tight to your body.

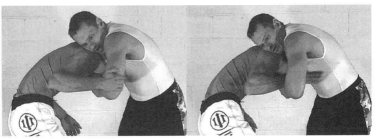

LINK 13
Fighter B: Pull to wedge
● Against a tight arm, use the wedge arm to cup his elbow and pull it toward you.
● Quickly insert your wedge inside the gap the pull opened up.

LINK 14
Fighter B: High crotch slam

● Leaving your wedge in place, step deep into Fighter A.
● Underhook his crotch with your free arm.
● Arch your back, look to the sky, lift your opponent and slam him to the mat. Follow with a cross-body ride.

LINK 15
Fighter B: Hammer the face

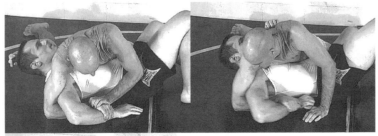

LINK 16
Fighter B: Hook a DWL

LINK 17
Fighter A: Trunk grab block

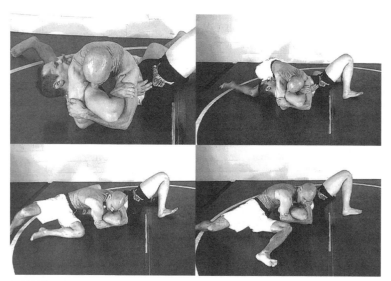

LINK 18
Fighter B: Keylock / Turn the corner short arm bar

● Beat the trunk grab with a key lock as shown above.

For the turn the corner short arm bar:
● Pop to your feet placing your head-side foot to the far side of his head.
● Place your hip-side foot on the near side of his body.
● Turn the corner toward his head, falling back for the short-arm bar.

Continued next page.

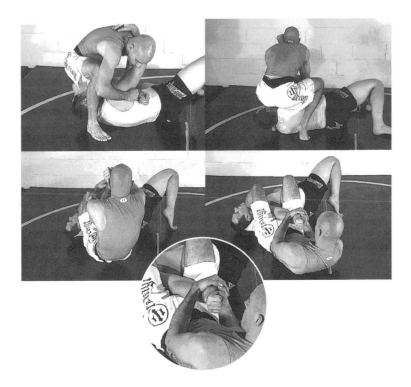

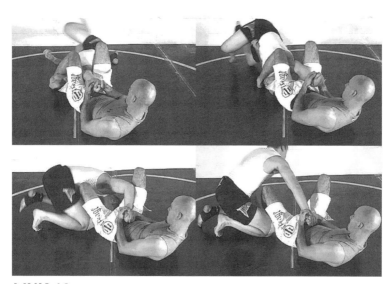

LINK 19
Fighter A: Outside roll

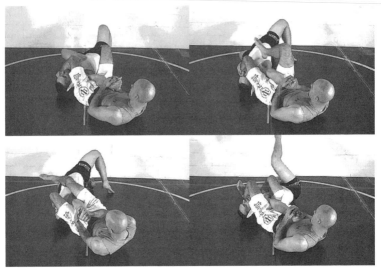

LINK 20
Fighter B: Follow to full arm bar

BAD LIB 8

Insert as LINK 14 in DRILL FIVE.

LINK 14
Fighter A: Crook lift and spin release
● Versus his wedge, cup his wedge elbow with the crook of your non-head attacking arm.
● Release your grip and lift his elbow while ...
● Shoving his head down with the back of your head-attack arm while ...
● Backstepping with your head-side foot and pivoting on your crook lift foot.

LINK 15
Fighter A: Lead hook
● Pop him as he ducks out of the spin release.
Fighter B: Cover

LINK 16
Fighter A: Cross
Fighter B: Cover

LINK 17
Fighter B: Shoot the double leg

LINK 18
Fighter A: Match level and bull post
● As Fighter B shoots, match his level and place both hands on his shoulders.

LINK 19
Fighter A: Short drag and outside step
● Use either hand (here, the left) to overhook his upper arm.
● Sling/drag his arm 45 degrees across his body while ...
● Stepping with your drag-side foot to the outside.

LINK 20
Fighter A: Shoot the double leg

BAD LIB 9

Here we'll insert another Bad Lib to the end of BAD LIB 8. Pick up where BAD LIB 8 left off at LINK 20.

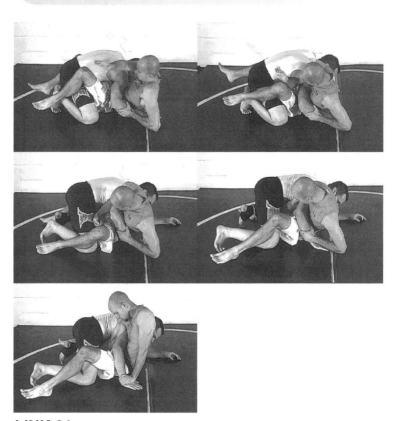

LINK 21
Fighter B: Armpit drag to switch

LINK 22
Fighter B: DWL
turnover to cross-body
DWL

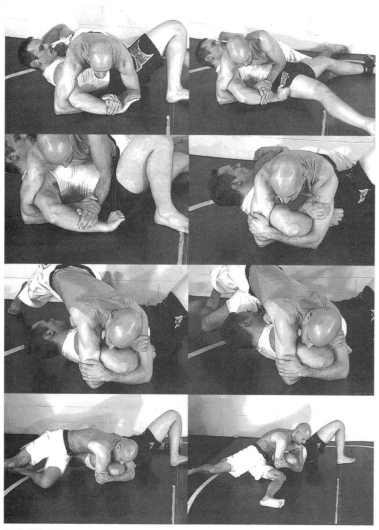

LINK 23
Fighter A: Trunk grab to block the DWL
Fighter B: Transition to keylock

DRILL SIX

LINK 1
Fighter A: Jab
Fighter B: Catch

LINK 2
Fighter B: Cross
Fighter A: Slip outside

LINK 3
Fighter B: Overhand off the slip
Fighter A: Cover

LINK 4
Fighter B: Hook
Fighter A: Cover

LINK 5
Fighter B: Shoot the double leg
● Hit the cross-body ride after hitting the mat.

LINK 6
Fighter B: Knees to
head

LINK 7
Fighter A: Cover and
post to block knees

NO

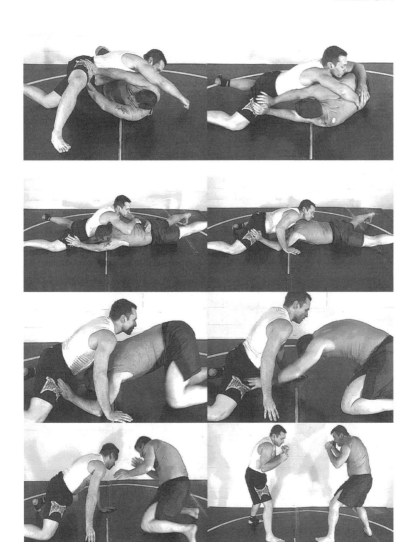

LINK 8
Fighter A: Belly down get-up
● Circle your hips away from Fighter B by posting on his hips with both hands.
● Go belly down and keep your hands on his hips.
● Get to your knees and return to standing.

LINK 9
Fighter A: Overhand
Fighter B: Cover

LINK 10
Fighter A: Double leg
● Gain cross-body ride position.

LINK 11
Fighter B: Bump to bottom scissors — guard

● Pop onto your near side.

● Post on his hip with your near elbow and your far hand.

● Scoot your hips away from him and then back in to bring your near knee between your bodies.

● Hook your bottom scissors.

LINK 12
Fighter A: Sit back tall

● In order to maintain good balance and to become resistant to sweeps and subs …

● Center your weight through your widespread knees and the balls of your feet.

● Sit up straight.

LINK 13
Fighter A: Overhand
Fighter B: Cover

LINK 14
Fighter A: Throw another overhand
Fighter B: Suck him in

● As Fighter A throws the overhand ...
● Use the forearm of the same side arm to block the punch while ...
● Using your legs to bring him in.
● Overhook his punching arm with your blocking arm.
● Grip the back of his neck with your other hand — notice this is collar and overhook position.
● Keep him broken down and tight to your body.

LINK 15
Fighter A: Hook body
● Use the free hand to hook his body.
Fighter B: Cover
● Maintain your head control and use the elbow of your head-control arm to block.
● You can assist this movement by slightly crunching toward the side being struck.

LINK 16
Fighter A: Hook head
Fighter B: Cover
● Keep your chin down and …
● Shrug your head control to cover.

LINK 17
Fighter A:
Hook body
Fighter B:
Establish a
knee / elbow
(bone wall)
block

● Maintain your overhook, but as he hooks the body ...

● Release your bottom scissors.

● Allow your head-control side elbow and knee to meet establishing a bone wall to block the punch.

LINK 18
Fighter B:
Bone wall to
post and
punch

● Once you've hit your bone wall ...

● Bring your overhook-side leg high on his back.

● Use your overhook limbs to get you more on your bone wall side.

● Maintain control of his "free" arm with your bone wall shin.

● Post on his face and shove with your bone wall hand.

● As he pushes back into you ...

● Remove your post and chop a quick punch to the face.

LINK 19
Fighter B: Transition to triangle
● Sneak your bone wall leg underneath his arm and bring it high and across his shoulder.
● Pop your hips into him and establish a figure-4 grip with your legs.
● Use your hips to bring him back in and drag his overhooked arm between your bodies.

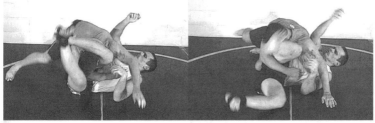

LINK 20
Fighter A: Sit-out versus triangle
● As soon as your overhooked arm has been dragged between your bodies ...
● In a burst, sit-out onto your free side hip as if you were going to sit on your dragged hand.
● While hitting the sit-out, you will be aggressively turning to face his legs.
● Gain cross-body.

LINK 21
Fighter A: Hammerfist head
● Take multiples — you earned it.
Fighter B: Cover

LINK 22
Fighter A: Grind face
● Place the head-side forearm on his head and grind.

LINK 23
Fighter A: Knee head
● Keep his head in place by scooping with the head-side palm.
● Sit out toward his head to give more heft to your knees.

DRILL SEVEN

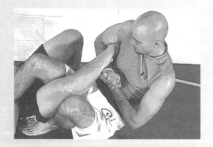

We'll hit a short chain here that introduces the high single and a leg lock attack and then branch a few more possibilities in short Bad Lib extensions.

LINK 1
Fighter A: Jab
Fighter B: Catch

LINK 2
Fighter A: Hook a high single leg
● See *NHBF: Takedowns* in this series for specific details.

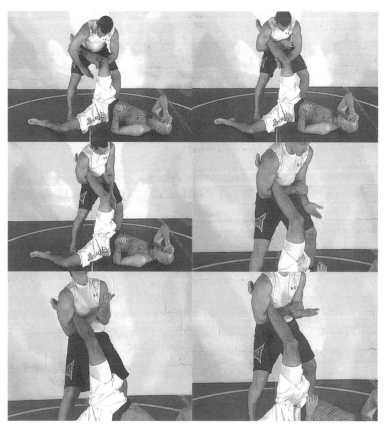

LINK 3
Fighter A: Hanging leg lock

● Once you've dumped him with the single leg ...

● Transfer his caught leg underneath your near arm (in this case his right leg under the right arm).

● Grip the forearm (not biceps) of your left arm with your right hand — a reverse lever grip (see **NHBF: The Ultimate Guide to Submission Wrestling** for details).

● Curl your left arm high while ...

● Stepping into him and ...

● Arching your back.

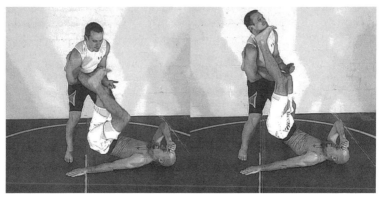

LINK 4
Fighter B: Kick / post with the free leg
● Use the free leg to deliver up-kicks or to post on Fighter A's hips to prevent his walking into you.

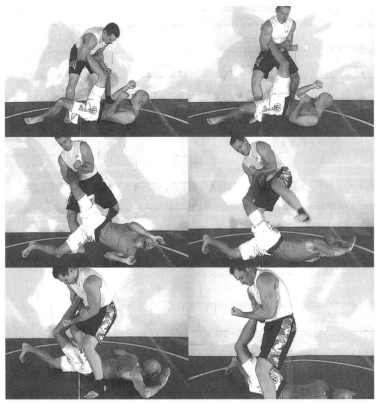

LINK 5
Fighter A: Jerk turn to 1/2 crab

● You might be surprised to see such a "pro/show" move included, but it hits h-a-r-d.

● Jerk/lift his leg as high as you can while you walk into him.

● Once he is stacked on his shoulders, jerk him toward his free-side shoulder (here, his left).

● As he turns belly-down, step over him with your left leg.

● Maintain your reverse lever.

● Sit back and crank his leg — sole of the foot toward the top of his head.

BAD LIB 10

Add as LINK 3 in DRILL SEVEN.

LINK 3
Fighter B: Wizzer and one-on-one
balance maintenance

● Versus Fighter A's high single, hook a wizzer on his near side arm (if he has your right leg, you wizzer the left arm and vice versa).
● Hop toward the attacked leg with your base foot.
● Grip his far wrist with your free hand.
● This is done to maintain balance.

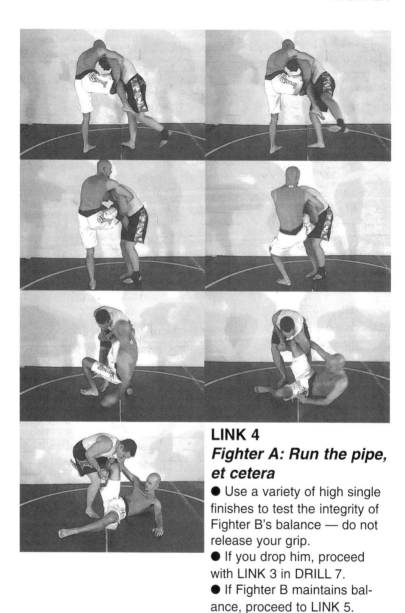

LINK 4
Fighter A: Run the pipe, et cetera

● Use a variety of high single finishes to test the integrity of Fighter B's balance — do not release your grip.

● If you drop him, proceed with LINK 3 in DRILL 7.

● If Fighter B maintains balance, proceed to LINK 5.

LINK 5
Fighter B: Head shove and sprawl

● Maintain your wizzer.

● Release the one-on-one grip and use that hand to shove his head down and to the inside.

● At the same time, sprawl your legs back while driving your weight through your wizzer contact point.

● Once you hit the mat, you will notice that you will be at the bottom of a collar and overhook, snapdown position. You may insert LINKS 9-13 from DRILL TWO here as a Bad Lib.

BAD LIB 11

Insert as LINK 4 in DRILL SEVEN.

LINK 4
Fighter B: Hook sweep

● Here, Fighter A has set up the hanging leg lock.
● Hook your free instep underneath Fighter A's free side leg (the leg on the side not attacking).
● Overhook his attacking-side heel with your attacked-side palm. ● Shove your attacked foot into him h-a-r-d while ...
● Kicking up and toward you with your elevator and ...
● Keeping his heel blocked with your hand.

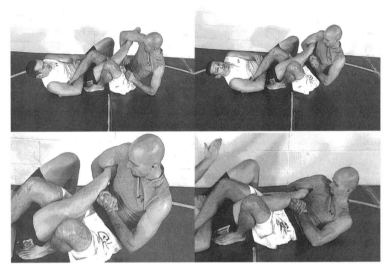

LINK 5
Fighter A: Lying Achilles lock
- As you fall, hook a guillotine grip.
- Squeeze your legs to stabilize his attacked leg.
- Curl/tighten your grip …
- While arching your hips hard.

LINK 6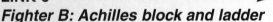
Fighter B: Achilles block and ladder
- Once you've hit him with the hook sweep …
- Shove your trapped leg deeper into his attacking overhook while pulling your toes back toward your shin — this provides a greater muscle mass and tightens this mass making it harder for him to finish as Achilles locks are more optimal closers to the ankle/heel.
- Use your hands to grab whatever rungs (body parts) are available and gain top position.

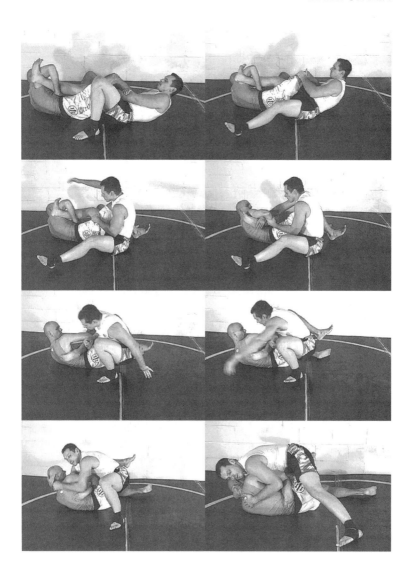

LINK 7
Fighter B: Reign down the strikes
● Once on top, fire punches and elbows to get the job done.

DRILL EIGHT

Here, we run a drill that features clinch work. For details on clinching foundations, see our volume in this series **NHBF: The Clinch**.

LINK 1
Fighter A: Jab
Fighter B: Catch

LINK 2
Fighter A: Jab
Fighter B: Catch and stick
● Catch the jab in the rear palm and drive off the rear foot to "follow" the jab back.
● Use your lead hand to muffle Fighter A's rear hand/arm.
● Seek an over-under clinch.

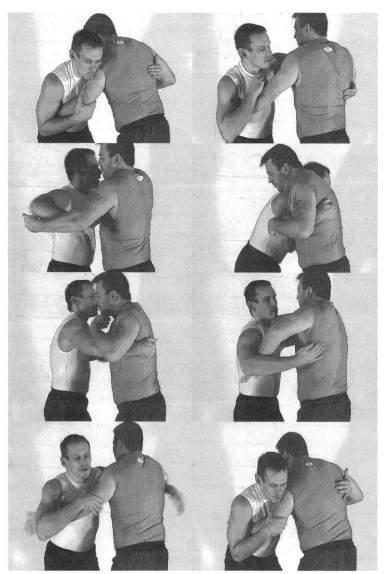

LINK 3
Fighter A and B: Pummel swim
● Once in the over-under position, hit two to three hard pummel/swim circuits.

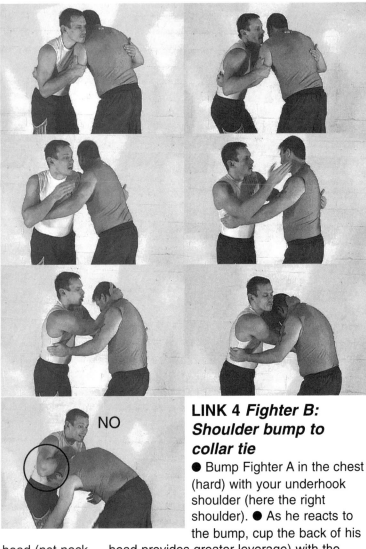

NO

LINK 4 *Fighter B: Shoulder bump to collar tie*

● Bump Fighter A in the chest (hard) with your underhook shoulder (here the right shoulder). ● As he reacts to the bump, cup the back of his head (not neck — head provides greater leverage) with the palm of your overhook hand. ● Jerk/pull his head down while keeping the collar tie elbow glued to his chest. Placing the elbow to the outside allows Fighter A to close the distance and attack.

LINK 5
Fighter B: Uppercut
● Keep your collar tie and fire an uppercut with your under-hook hand.

LINK 6
Fighter B: Hook
● Add a hook with the uppercut hand.

LINK 7
Fighter B: Establish a double collar tie-up
● Cup both hands on the back of his head (again, not neck).
● Jerk/pull his head down while keeping your elbows between your bodies.

LINK 8
Fighter B: Rear clinch knee

LINK 9 *Fighter B: Lead skip knee*

LINK 10 *Fighter B: Rear skip knee*

LINK 11
Fighter B: Double collar tie-up to halch to bar and chancery

● Jerk his head low.
● Remove your top hand (here the left) while keeping the other hand in place.
● Step toward the removed hand side.
● Stack your left hand on top of your right hand — entering from the right side.
● Stack your chin on top of your hands.
● Use all three limbs (both hands and chin) to keep his head low.
● Overhook his head with your right arm.
● Underhook his right arm with your left arm to establish the bar and chancery position.

LINK 12
Fighter B: Round knee

● This knee is delivered with the inside of the knee as described in our volume *NHBF: Savage Strikes*.

LINK 13
Fighter B: Bar and chancery drop

● Pull down on his head with your right arm.
● Lift his right arm with your left.
● Back step with your right foot and drop him to the mat.
● Follow him, keeping your hooks in place and blanket him.

LINK 14
Fighter B: Bar and chancery to chin hook crank

● If you are able to hook his chin (molars) with your head-control hand at the top end of the bar and chancery — do so.

● Once on the mat, sit-out toward his head while pulling his chin.

● Pull down on his right shoulder for the contrary motion required to finish.

LINK 15
Fighter B: Bar and chancery drop to flat crank

● Hit this one when you don't have a chin hook.

● At the bottom of the bar and chancery drop, sprawl and blanket him.

● Wrap your head-control arm tighter.

● Keep him pressured to the mat and on his back as much as you can manage.

● Use the contrary motion shoulder pull on his far shoulder while arching and looking over your head-side shoulder.

● Do not roll and lift his upper back off of the mat — a common error.

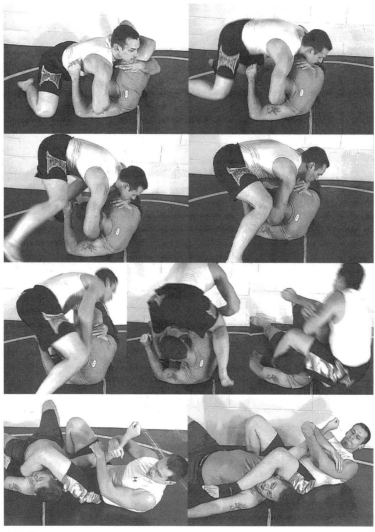

LINK 16
Fighter B: Short arm bar

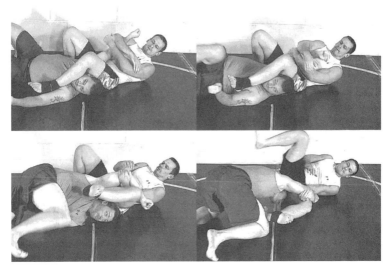

LINK 17 *Fighter A: Outside roll*

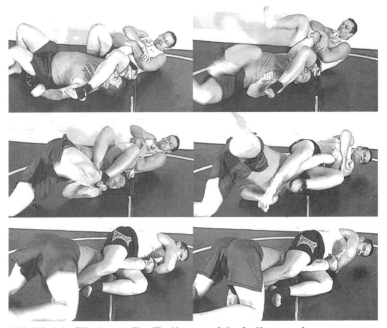

LINK 18 *Fighter B: Follow with full arm bar*

BAD LIB 12

Add as LINK 12 in DRILL EIGHT.

LINK 12
Fighter A: Step into the hole
● As Fighter A attempts the bar and chancery drop, step toward the direction he is trying to drop you in order to stalemate.

LINK 13 *Fighter B: Head snap*

● As Fighter A resists your bar and chancery drop, grip his chin with your head-control hand. ● Grip the back of his head with your underhook hand. ● Quickstep back as you pull/jerk his head 45 degrees and down.

LINK 14

At this point we could transition to DRILL TWO, LINK 9 to continue this Bad Lib, but we'll use a different go-behind to educate a new skill. We'll use a go-behind that doesn't presume overhook control.

Fighter B: Head post go-behind ➤

● Post your chin hook hand (here, the right hand) on top of his head and keep him shoved down. ● Begin moving toward your right (his left). ● As you turn the corner, replace your post with your left hand. ● It is vital to keep your posts in place until you have completed your go-behind. A good player will surge, drive, catch a leg or easily pull guard at this point. Your job is to make that as difficult as possible.

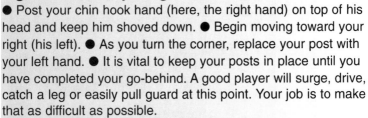

LINK 15

Now Fighter B will pick up from LINK 11 in DRILL TWO and run it to the end to finish this Bad Lib.

BAD LIB 13

We add this sequence as LINK 8 in DRILL EIGHT.

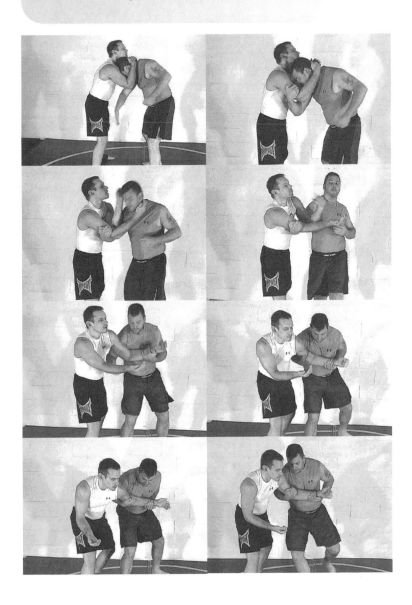

LINK 8
Fighter A: Double-up shrug beat versus double collar tie-up to outside Russian

● Shrug your right shoulder hard into his left arm while snapping your head to the left.
● At the same time, reach under both of his arms with your right and grip his right triceps.
● Use your leftt hand to reach over the top of his arms and grip his left forearm.
● As you finish the shrug, transfer your grips. Your right hand will underhook and grip his left upper arm.
● Your right will underhook and grip his left forearm.
● You will plaster your right shoulder on his left upper arm.

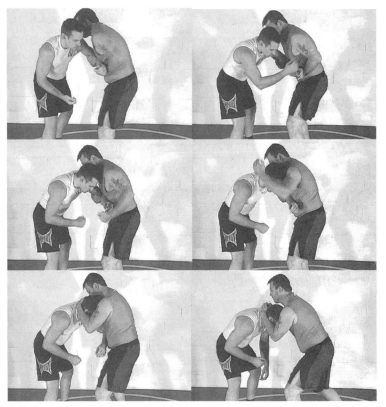

LINK 9
Fighter A: Hook a double collar tie-up
● Step your left foot in front of his body.
● Cup the back of his head with your left hand and jerk his head.
● Now, double-up with your right hand.

LINK 10
Fighter A: Rear knee

LINK 11
Fighter A: Elbow
- Release your top hand and fire the elbow to the head.
- Reestablish the clinch.

LINK 12
Fighter B: Hip post
- Place both hands on his hips and attempt to get tall. This will block both his knees and stop him from breaking you down.

LINK 13
Fighter B: Uppercut

LINK 14
Fighter B: Corkscrew hook
● Fire the hook at a 45 degree and down angle over his clinch.

LINK 15
Fighter B: Double-up shrug
● Return the favor with a double-up shrug.

LINK 16
Fighter B: Overhand
● As soon as you have the tie-up break, fire the overhand.

BAD LIB 14

Add as Link 4 in DRILL EIGHT.

LINK 4
Fighter B: Body lock crunch

● Here, we assume you won the pummel war and secured a body lock.

● Plaster your head on his chest while you tighten your grip.

● Step to the side away from the direction you're facing.

● Jerk his hips toward you while using your head against his chest to crunch him to the mat.

● Follow him to the mat and hit a top saddle/mounted position.

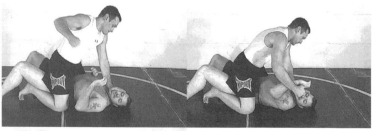

LINK 5
Fighter B: Face / neck post punch and elbow

LINK 6
Fighter B: Shoulder choke

Statistically it is wiser to take the win with the ground and pound, but for the sake of drilling useful skills, we continue this chain.

● Use your striking hand to knock his same side arm across his face (right versus left and vice versa).

● Collapse to trap his arm across his face while …

● Encircling his head with your post arm.

● Hit a reverse lever grip and hop to cross-body on his arm trap side.

● Tighten your grip to finish.

Continued next page.

LINK 7
Fighter A: Leg hug shoulder choke stalemate

LINK 8
Fighter B: Pop-up to short arm bar

- Release your reverse lever grip.
- Keep his arm and post on his face yet again with the same post hand.
- Pop up placing your hip-side shin in his back and …
- Your head-side foot over his face.
- Take the short arm bar.

LINK 9
Fighter A: Outside roll

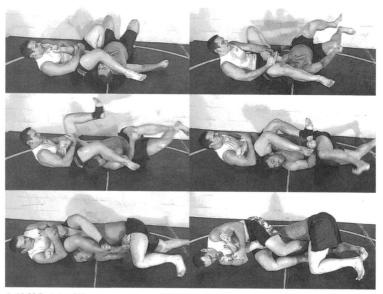

LINK 10 *Fighter B: Follow to full arm bar*

BAD LIB 15

Add BAD LIB 15 to BAD LIB 14 at LINK 6.

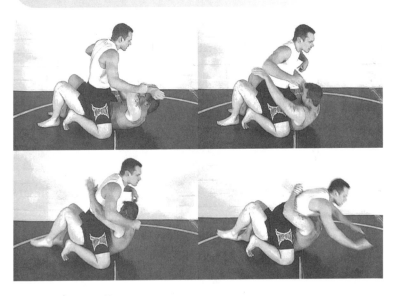

LINK 6
Fighter A: Bridge and hug
● To buy some time versus a ground and pound assault ...
● Hit a boxer's position with both arms.
● Hit a high, fast bridge.
● As your opponent is brought forward, hug him tightly at the waist and bury your face into his body to hide from the blows.

LINK 7
Fighter A: Press bridge top saddle/mount escape
● Release your body lock and quickly post both hands on his hips — fingers facing to the outside.
● Pop a high bridge while simultaneously "bench pressing" him skyward.
● Bring one knee between his legs — here the right knee.
● Use your three posts (both hands and single knee) to push him toward your knee side.
● As soon as he hits the mat, begin shrimping/scrambling to better position.

Continued next page.

LINK 8
Fighter A: Heel hook
● Once Fighter B is dumped … ● Overhook his top leg with your top leg. ● Drive your overhook heel into his stomach while squeezing your knees together.
● Hook the back of your top hand (not crook of the arm — too much sweat for good gripping) underneath his caught heel.
● Hit a palm-to-palm grip.
● Torque his heel toward your body's midline to tap.

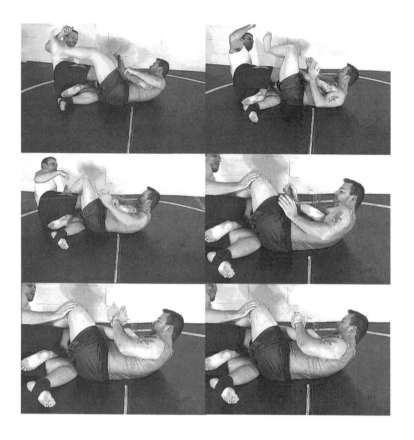

Conclusion

There is no way to provide a definitive conclusion on this subject of hybridized MMA drilling. The drills presented here are (literally) the tip of the iceberg. As we have demonstrated, each individual link within a given drill is fissionable material — meaning that each link can morph into any given number of its own drill chains.

While not a definitive drill book, this primer does provide you with more than enough tools to break down the walls of compartmentalization and move you well down the road toward complete integration. At a later date, we will provide even more drills and drill subsets.

In the meantime, take these drills and grasp the wisdom of integrating all aspects of the fight into single training loops. Loops that are informed, not by personal preference, but by what actually occurs under competitive circumstances. Adhere to the training protocol that commands you to always start each drill round with link 1 realizing that by the "end" of any given drill chain, you will have inculcated the high percentage material at the front of the chain by sheer dint of forced repetition. It is this sort of "stacked deck" hybrid drilling that will forge you into the new breed of fighter who is the jack-of-all-trades and links all upon a single thread.

I wish you every success in your training. If there is anything I can do to assist, please let me know via

www.extremeselfprotection.com

Train hard, train safe, train smart!

Mark Hatmaker

Resources

BEST CHOICES

First, please visit my Web site at
www.extremeselfprotection.com
You will find even more training
material as well as updates and
other resources.

Amazon.com

The place to browse for books such
as this one and other similar titles.

Paladin Press
www.paladin-press.com

Paladin carries many training
resources as well as some of my
videos, which allow you to see
much of what is covered in my
NHB books.

Ringside Boxing
www.ringside.com

Best choice for primo equipment.

Sherdog.com

Best resource for MMA news, event
results and NHB happenings.

Threat Response Solutions
www.trsdirect.com

They also offer many training
resources along with some of my
products.

Tracks Publishing
www.startupsports.com

They publish all the books in the
NHBF series as well as a few fine
boxing titles.

www.humankinetics.com

Training and conditioning info.

www.matsmatsmats.com

Best resource for quality mats at
good prices.

Video instruction

Extreme Self-Protection
extremeselfprotection.com

Paladin Press
paladin-press.com

Threat Response Solutions
trsdirect.com

World Martial Arts
groundfighter.com

Events

IFC
ifc-usa.com

IVC
valetudo.com

King of the Cage
kingofthecage.com

Pancrase
so-net.ne.jp/pancrase

Pride
pridefc.com

The Ultimate Fighting
Championships
ufc.tv

Universal Combat Challenge
ucczone.ca/

Index

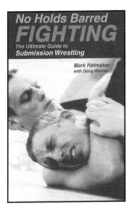

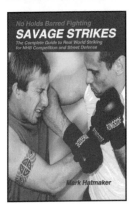

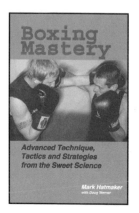

Boxing Mastery
Advance Techniques, Tactics and Strategies from the Sweet Science
Advanced boxing skills and ring generalship.
1-884654-21-5 / $12.95
900 photos

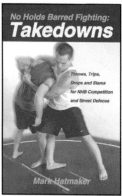

No Holds Barred Fighting: Takedowns
Throws, Trips, Drops and Slams for NHB Competition and Street Defense
1-884654-25-8 / $12.95
850 photos

No Holds Barred Fighting: The Clinch
Offensive and Defensive Concepts Inside NHB's Most Grueling Position
1-884654-27-4 / $12.95
750 photos

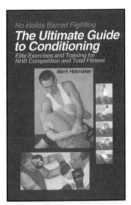

No Holds Barred Fighting:
The Ultimate Guide to Conditioning
Elite Exercises and Training for NHB
Competition and Total Fitness
1-884654-29-0 / $12.95
900 photos

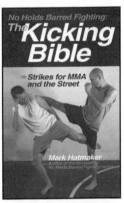

No Holds Barred Fighting:
The Kicking Bible
Strikes for MMA and the Street
1-884654-31-2 / $12.95
700 photos

No Second Chance:
A Reality-Based Guide to Self-Defense
How to avoid and survive an assault.
1-884654-32-0 / $12.95
500 photos

No Holds Barred Fighting:
The Book of Essential Submissions
How MMA champions gain their victories. A catalog of winning submissions.
1-884654-27-4 / $12.95
750 photos

MMA Mastery: Flow Chain Drilling
and Integrated O/D Training
to Submission Wrestling
Blendis all aspects of the MMA fight game into devastating performances.
1-884654-38-x / $13.95
800 photos

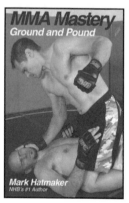

MMA Mastery: Ground and Pound
A comprehensive guide to the ground game.
1-884654-39-8 / $13.95
650 photos

Mark Hatmaker is the bestselling author of the *No Holds Barred Fighting Series,* the *MMA Mastery Series, No Second Chance* and *Boxing Mastery.* He also has produced more than 40 instructional videos. His resume includes extensive experience in the combat arts including boxing, wrestling, Jiu-jitsu and Muay Thai.

He is a highly regarded coach of professional and amateur fighters, law enforcement officials and security personnel. Hatmaker founded Extreme Self Protection (ESP), a research body that compiles, analyzes and teaches the most effective Western combat methods known. ESP holds numerous seminars throughout the country each year including the prestigious Karate College/Martial Arts Universities in Radford, Virginia. He lives in Knoxville, Tennessee.